A GUIDE TO OVERCOMING

CONSTIPATION AND STOOL WITHHOLDING

IN CHILDREN

KATHLEEN M. DIEHL

Also by Kathleen M. Diehl:

The Collective Awakening (2009)

Beyond Disease Care (2011)

A GUIDE TO OVERCOMING

CONSTIPATION AND STOOL WITHHOLDING

IN CHILDREN

GATEWAY TO BEING

KATHLEEN M. DIEHL

GATEWAY TO BEING

Published and distributed by: Gateway to Being
gatewaytobeing@cox.net
Cover design by: Kathleen M. Diehl
Illustrations by: Kathleen M. Diehl
www.kathleendiehl.com

CONTENTS

III: HOW DO WE STOP THIS?

5. Introduction to Treatment Options

6. The "Magic Combination"

7. Alternative Protocols

APPENDICES

INTRODUCTION

by Kathleen M. Diehl

"Stool withholding." It might seem like an odd or even embarrassing topic to most, but if you're raising a child who is bound and determined to do everything in his power to avoid having a bowel movement, you understand what I mean when I say it's now become the most important topic in your home. When my own family became faced with this hellish ordeal, there were no books on the market to guide us. We had never even *heard* of stool withholding, and we certainly didn't know any other families who were going through it.

For some children, stool withholding is just an occasional inconvenience that passes relatively quickly. For others, stool withholding becomes a chronic and severely traumatizing ordeal that can persist for a *very* long time. If your child falls in the latter category, the importance of addressing this problem with your undivided attention cannot be overstated. Left to go on for weeks, months or years, the stool withholding cycle can be very damaging, causing longstanding physical, psychological and emotional effects.

I am the mother of two wonderful boys, one who is now grown and the other a sophomore in high school. Around the age of three, one of my sons (I won't name names) passed a large, constipated stool, after which he decided that pooping *hurt* and he wasn't going to do it anymore! Little did we know we were about to enter into a nightmare from which we may never fully awaken. Things became *so* desperate for *so* long, we probably would have paid any price for a safe and effective solution.

I remember our little boy's unstoppable determination to hold it in, despite all my and his father's attempts to rationalize with (and even bribe) him. I remember the build-up of anxiety in our home as yet another day would come and go without a bowel movement. I remember the sheer trauma of the "big event" when he could no longer avoid the inevitable. I remember the helplessness we felt watching our terrified child scream, cry and kick his legs in pain while we held him on the toilet and coached him to "let it out, let it out." And, who could forget the trip to the emergency room when he began to vomit from severe impaction after managing to withhold for a record nine days!

In other words, I've been there. As a parent, you may wonder whether your child has some kind of complex psychological or emotional problem, or, begin to suspect this whole scenario is somehow your fault (neither of which are likely true). You're *desperate* to do whatever it takes to help your child overcome this, but I'm guessing you've heard some pretty scary things about "laxatives" and you really aren't sure what to do or who to trust—including your pediatrician.

Despite the fact that stool withholding is a relatively common issue in preschool-age children, there seems to be a lot of conflicting opinions in the medical community. Some doctors take it seriously, explaining to parents the importance of having and following a comprehensive plan; others send families home with nothing more than a prescription. Then, when parents read the patient information sheet from the pharmacy or look the prescription up online, they are concerned to see: "Do not use for more than two weeks" or "Not for use in children under the age of 6." Who *wouldn't* question its safety or be afraid to use it? The Internet has several articles on treatment options, but there doesn't appear to be any clear, uniting consensus.

Trust me, I feel your pain. I know *exactly* what your family has been going through, and I'm here to help. This book contains the most comprehensive information available on childhood constipation and stool withholding, all of which is backed by physician advice, personal experience, research and references. You will learn what causes stool withholding, what complications can develop, what treatment options are available, the importance of addressing lifestyle factors, how to create a fail-proof plan *and* how to get your child to cooperate without a battle.*

My goal is to give you the knowledge and tools necessary to create a safe and effective individualized plan of action that will ensure both short and long-term success. Before making any major changes to your child's routine, be sure to have all your "ducks in a row." Read this book from cover to cover, use the checklist provided in Appendix A, gather all your supplies and enlist the support of family and caregivers. As an old Proverb states, "He who fails to plan, plans to fail."[1] Let's begin!

* WARNING: The information in this book does not constitute medical advice. Be sure to consult with your child's pediatrician before starting or discontinuing any treatment plan.

SECTION I

HOW DID WE GET HERE?

NOTE: To avoid writing "he/she" and "him/her," the author will use he/him throughout the book when referring to your stool-withholding child.

CHAPTER 1

DEFINING CONSTIPATION

What Is Constipation?

Stool withholding begins with constipation. To summarize and simplify the various definitions that are out there, this book will define "constipation" as stools that are: 1) infrequent, 2) hardened or dry, 3) difficult to pass and/or 4) incomplete. In other words, the bowels just aren't running regularly, smoothly or comfortably.

When a young child is constipated, he is likely to be fussy, whiny and disagreeable. If you've ever suffered from constipation as an adult, you know the miserable effect it can have on your everyday life. Just because constipation is so very *common* in modern society doesn't mean it is *normal*—and it certainly doesn't mean it is *healthy*.

Constipation often results in far more than just stomach aches, indigestion, nausea, bloating and a feeling of fullness. As my trusted local chiropractor often tells me, when the body's wastes and toxins aren't being efficiently eliminated, you may also experience poor immunity (and resulting frequent infections such as colds and flu), brain fog, mood swings, allergies, inflammation, headaches, fatigue, depression and many other uncomfortable symptoms too numerous to list.[1]

American Academy of Pediatrics Normal Bowel Movement Frequency Chart

AGE	BMs PER WK	BMs PER DAY
0-3 mos.		
breast-fed	5-40	2.9
formula-fed	5-40	2.0
6-12 mos.	5-28	1.8
1-3 yrs.	4-21	1.4
over 3 yrs.	3-14	1.0

The above chart details the typical bowel movement frequency for infants and young children.[2] As you can see, there is a large variation in what's considered "normal." Although some experts claim that having a bowel movement every other day or every third day is perfectly normal for some people, most holistic health professionals would disagree. For good health, abundant energy and an overall sense of well-being, most holistic practitioners recommend having 1-3 large bowel movements per day—preferably one after each meal.[3]

FOOD IN

⬇

WASTE OUT

Perhaps the best parameter of a healthy bowel movement frequency for any individual is, "How do you feel?" If your answer is "sluggish and irritable," there's a good chance constipation is at least partially to blame.

Regardless of frequency, stools should be soft and easy to pass without straining or discomfort. Many experts say stool should be shaped much like a long torpedo, whereas others say softer, unformed pieces are best. If stools are watery, you have the opposite problem—diarrhea.

Constipation Causes

Constipation is a *symptom*, it is not a disease or disorder in and of itself. As you likely know, constipation in adults is usually caused by lifestyle factors such as inadequate water intake, a refined, low-fiber diet and/or a lack of exercise.[4]

Likewise, when a young child suffers from constipation, he often fits the profile of a strong-willed child who refuses to drink plain water, refuses to eat natural, whole foods and leads a relatively inactive lifestyle (for example, spending most of the day in front of the television or computer screen).*

It's common to experience constipation or irregularity during times of stress or major changes in routine (such as travelling, starting a new school, etc). Constipation can also occur as a side effect of various medications, or, as the result of unrecognized food allergies or hypersensitivities.

* For tips on how to get your child to drink plain water, eat natural, high-fiber whole foods and engage in active play, see Chapters 9-11.

When we think of food allergies, we usually think of sudden, obvious symptoms such as hives, swelling or difficulty breathing. However, the vast majority of food reactions are much more difficult to discern! Undetected food hypersensitivities can cause anything from headaches to eczema to depression.[5]

The two most common food proteins causing hypersensitivity reactions are *casein* (the protein found in milk) and *gluten* (the protein found in wheat, rye, barley and cross-contaminated oats). Even if your child seems fine both before and after consuming these foods (no direct or immediate reaction), it is worth considering a two-week dietary elimination to determine whether this alone reverses his chronic constipation.*

In rare cases, constipation may be a symptom of a more serious disorder, such as congenital structural abnormalities, neurodevelopmental delay, celiac disease, Hirschprung's disease, hypothyroidism, cystic fibrosis, multiple sclerosis, Parkinson's disease, spinal cord injuries, colon cancer, diabetes or heavy metal toxicity.[6] Any such suspicion warrants a consultation with a pediatrician or other trusted health practitioner.

This book addresses the problem of functional constipation. "Functional constipation" refers to constipation that has no *physiological* cause. According to Stephen Borowitz, MD, functional constipation is most likely to begin at three key times in a child's life—times of significant transition.

---

* For more information on food hypersensitivities and how to properly perform a 2-week dietary elimination trial, please see my other book, *Beyond Disease Care*, co-authored with Walt Stoll, MD.

The first key time is during infancy, either at the time of weaning, transitioning from breast milk to formula, transitioning to cow's milk and/or introducing solid foods. The second key time is when the parents initiate toilet training (especially bowel training). The third is when the child enters school, as he may have anxiety and hesitation with using an unfamiliar bathroom.[7]

Finally, certain personality types just seem to be more prone to bowel issues than others. The most curious and adventurous little ones are having way too much fun exploring to want to stop and sit on the toilet when that "gotta go" feeling comes along. The really clever ones figure out how to wrap their exhausted parents around their tiny little fingers, engaging in power struggles and drama over toilet training or transitioning from diapers to "big-kid pants." On the other side of the coin, some of the more sensitive and timid ones may be genuinely afraid of using public restrooms or flushing a part of themselves down the toilet. The potential contributing factors are many.

A Quick Anatomy Lesson

To better understand how constipation actually occurs, it is helpful to learn the basics about what the gastrointestinal (G.I.) tract is, and does. The G.I. tract is basically one long, continuous tube that begins at the mouth and ends at the anus. It includes the mouth, esophagus, stomach, duodenum, small intestine, large intestine, rectum and anus.[8] The inside of your mouth is, technically, outside your body. So too, the inside of the intestinal tract is, technically, outside your body. Interesting, isn't it?

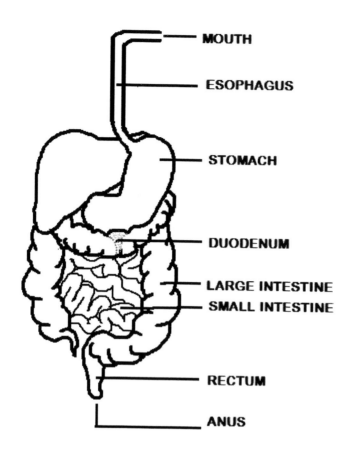

MOUTH

ESOPHAGUS

STOMACH

DUODENUM

LARGE INTESTINE
SMALL INTESTINE

RECTUM

ANUS

The small and large intestines undergo muscular contractions (known as "peristalsis" or the "gastrocolic reflex") several times per day, keeping food and wastes running downward through the digestive system. This is the cause of that sudden urge you feel after eating (or having your morning caffeine). Whether or not you heed Nature's call is more or less voluntary, as we have all learned how to postpone or ignore the sensation when it's inconvenient or there's just no bathroom available.

As you probably already know, one of the main functions of the G.I. tract is to digest food, extract vital nutrients and eliminate waste. The amount of time it takes for a food you have eaten to travel through the G.I. tract and exit the body is known as the "transit time." A simple way to determine your transit time is to eat some corn and see how long it takes to show up in your stool. When stool moves too slowly through the colon for whatever reason, water gets absorbed from the stool back into the body, resulting in dry, hard, constipated stools.

Of course, *prevention* is the best medicine for any health complaint, and childhood constipation is no exception. However, since you are actually interested in reading a book by this title, I'm guessing it's probably too late for that. You've already learned the hard way that when constipation leads to even *one* single episode of an oversized, difficult to pass and painful stool, the stage is set for the vicious cycle of stool withholding—the topic of our next chapter.

CHAPTER 2

THE STOOL WITHHOLDING CYCLE

What Is Stool Withholding?

As mentioned previously, stool withholding begins with constipation. Stool withholding means just as its name says—purposely holding stool (poop) inside instead of letting it out when the urge comes. Some children manage to withhold stool for 3-7 days at a time (my own son managed even longer). Meanwhile, the stool is becoming larger and larger inside the colon. When it finally passes, it can be extremely painful and *frightening* for the child. Thus, a vicious cycle of pain, fear and avoidance begins.

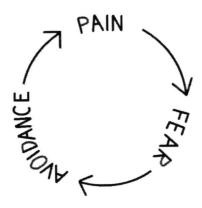

Once a young child has experienced this type of unexpected trauma, his natural response is, **"Pooping hurts! I'm never going to let *that* happen again!"** What began as an unexpected single episode may well turn into a conscious, determined, all-out commitment to hold all subsequent bowel movements in from now 'til the end of time. Adults know this approach would never work, but young children often do not.

Parents often have *no idea* their child is constipated until things have reached the unfortunate stage of stool withholding. During the first few years of my own son's life, he had the opposite problem—stools that were too runny—so constipation wasn't exactly on our radar. Of course, when a child is in diapers, it's easy to keep track of his bowel movements. But once he is using the bathroom independently, you may not realize there's a problem brewing until the screaming begins!

How Common Is Stool Withholding?

Stool withholding is a highly sensitive subject, and I can't help but wonder how many families are suffering in silence. It is difficult to gather accurate statistics on just how common this problem is, but I have seen estimates that between 20-30% of young children go through this to one degree or another. Of those who do, almost a third will suffer for at least six months and/or develop severe withholding requiring behavioral and laxative intervention.

One study conducted by Bruce Taubman, MD involved 482 healthy, urine-trained children between 18-30 months old. The objective was to determine the incidence of bowel training refusal and identify risk factors. Of the 482 children, 106 (22%) experienced bowel training refusal for one month or more. Of this number, most were nearing four years of age. Intervention had to be taken with 29 children due to severe withholding.[1]

With something this common and this impactful on so many family's lives, it is amazing to me that even today in 2011 I could find only *one* book on the market written specifically for parents dealing with this issue, and it didn't exactly have glowing reviews. Clearly, a more comprehensive guide is desperately needed, especially since so few pediatricians seem to be taking an active role in helping families prevent and resolve this vexing problem.

Even during annual well-child visits, many pediatricians fail to question parents about their child's bowel movement frequency and consistency once the child reaches preschool. Fewer yet take the time to educate parents on the importance of diet and exercise, or the potential warning signs of withholding.

Signs of Withholding

One tell-tale sign of longstanding constipation is "soiling" (encopresis). Soiling is the involuntary seepage of watery fecal matter into the child's underpants, caused by a build-up of stool (impaction).[2] Soiling is sometimes mistaken for "having an accident," but I can assure you soiling is out of your child's control. Rather than scolding and punishing, view these events for what they are—evidence of severe constipation, withholding due to pain, or both.

Another very clear tell-tale sign your child is withholding is the various physical postures and movements he makes when the urge comes and he frantically starts doing everything in his power to keep the stool from coming out. You will see rocking, squatting, stiffening, hiding, bottom clenching, leg crossing, back arching, forward hunching, strange dancing, toe or heel walking and more! These behaviors combined with panic and crying are very clear signs your child has been recently affected by a very painful bowel movement.

If your child is soiling or displaying any of the withholding behaviors just described, consider whether he might be having severe bowel training anxiety. Some children do fine with urine training, but just aren't ready to do "number two" in the toilet or potty chair.

Big Kid Pants Versus Diapers

If your child's stool withholding pattern seems to be connected to bowel training anxiety, consider going back to diapers on a temporary basis. In my experience, when a child develops a strong fear of *anything*, it has the potential to override *everything* (including all your attempts at bribery and logic!). The excitement of wearing "big girl" and "big boy" pants just isn't enough when a child isn't ready or doesn't feel safe. Until or unless that changes, any efforts toward potty training goals are likely to backfire.

Jessica Williams, a mom who has been through the stool withholding ordeal with one of her own sons, states: "Our son was so afraid of releasing stool into the toilet that he would hold it in until he had a diaper on. In the beginning, we refused to give him a diaper because we felt it would be 'back sliding.' Without a diaper, he would hold it for days until he suddenly became sick to his stomach and the urge to have a bowel movement was so great that he could no longer control it. By this time, he would have such a large, hard stool to pass that he would scream and be in incredible pain. Coaching him through one of these movements was like coaching a woman in labor—you knew the pain was incredible and there was nothing you could do."[3]

If you have more than one child, you know that each child has his own unique personality and disposition, and each child develops at his own pace. Just because your child's siblings, cousins and classmates were fully potty trained by age three doesn't mean your child has to be. This is not a "now or never" situation. Unless he has a specific disability presenting a unique obstacle, do you really think your child will not be fond of the idea of reporting to first grade in a diaper?

Comparisons will get you nowhere. Compassion and understanding, however, can go a very long way. Now is the time to *let go of worrying about what other people think* (including the mother-in-law), and focus on doing what's best for your child—who just so happens to be facing a very challenging situation. If easing his fear and getting him to "go" means reverting back to diapers for now, then so be it. Remember, "What you resist, persists!"

The next section will explore some of the common complications that can develop when constipation and stool withholding are not properly and consistently addressed. Hopefully none of these complications have occurred with your child thus far, but if they have, it is even more urgent that you work with your doctor to get the problem under control immediately.

SECTION II

WHAT ARE THE RISKS?

CHAPTER 3

FISSURES AND HEMORRHOIDS

What Is an Anal Fissure?

Passing an extremely over-sized stool—even once—puts your child at risk for a common complication known as an "anal fissure." An anal fissure is a painful, semi-permanent split or tear in the skin of the anus or anal canal. Anal fissures can occur in infants as well as children and adults. Initial signs and symptoms include a sudden, sharp pain when passing stool (may be severe, with significant crying and distress), and often, rectal bleeding (bright red blood on stool, diaper or toilet paper).

An anal fissure warrants an office visit to your child's pediatrician. Upon examination, the physician may find a visible crack, lump or skin tag on the skin of the anus.[1] He or she will likely advise you to take steps toward preventing ongoing constipation, such as administering stool softeners and/or laxatives, and increasing fluids and dietary fiber. Of course, these are the same guidelines presented in this book.

Once a fissure is present, there's likely to be significant anal itching and irritation, which may be partially relieved by sitting in a warm bath, applying cool compresses and soothing the area with petroleum jelly or a zinc oxide ointment.[2] A damp washcloth wrapped around a small baggie of frozen peas works very well as a cool compress.

If your child doesn't already have an anal fissure, hopefully this chapter will motivate you to prevent one. All it takes is one hard, oversized stool to tear the anus. Anal fissures are not only painful, but difficult to heal. As with any split in the skin, you must avoid pulling the edges apart during the healing process. If your child already has a fissure, it is *more important than ever* to ensure that each and every bowel movement is soft and easy to pass in order to make complete healing possible. By following the guidelines in this book, or the protocol recommended by your child's physician, a new anal fissure will usually heal in about two weeks.

Unfortunately, any fissure that does not heal within 6-8 weeks (due to repeated large, hard stools) may require surgical repair. This procedure is known as a "fissurectomy." When properly performed by a skilled surgeon, and when post-op instructions for laxative use are carefully followed, the success rate of cure is very high. One study reported 81% of children were asymptomatic six weeks after the procedure. Of the 11% still experiencing symptoms, most admitted failure to follow the surgeon's post-op guidelines.[3]

Kids Get Hemorrhoids, Too

A more common and less serious (but still seriously annoying) complication of chronic constipation is the almighty "hemorrhoid." Hemorrhoids (also known as "piles") are swollen, irritated veins in the rectum or along the anus. Although usually associated with adults, they can occur at any age—even in an infant—if constipation is present. Symptoms include pain, itching and sometimes, bleeding.

Hemorrhoids may be external or internal, and they usually develop as a result of pressure and straining. They are extremely common, for example, in a woman who has just given birth. Once present, they tend to go through alternating periods of remission and exacerbation.

External hemorrhoids may be a deep purple color. If there are several, they may look like a cluster of small dark grapes. Internal hemorrhoids often go unnoticed until or unless they begin to protrude out of the anus (prolapse)—which can be very uncomfortable and possibly lead to strangulation in the vein.

The only way to truly prevent hemorrhoids is to avoid the factors that create them in the first place. The lifestyle guidelines in this book will ensure bowel movements occur regularly and effortlessly. Once hemorrhoids are already present, it is possible for the veins to shrink back to normal size if they are not being repeatedly strained. Some severe and/or longstanding hemorrhoids may require specialized treatment such as surgical removal (hemorrhoidectomy), banding, laser or other techniques.

If your child has hemorrhoids, you may ease the symptoms the same way as instructed for anal fissures. Let him sit and play in a warm bath or apply cool compresses. As long as you are doing what it takes to prevent ongoing constipation, chances are the problem will be short-lived and full healing will occur. If he is in ongoing distress, or if bleeding is present, see your pediatrician.

Of course, both fissures and hemorrhoids greatly exacerbate the original problem, perpetuating the pain, fear and avoidance cycle. Children who develop either of these complications will undoubtedly *increase* their determination to withhold in an attempt to avoid further trauma. It is important to *make solving this problem your full-time job*, because your child may already be at higher risk for developing the more serious complications described in the next chapter.

CHAPTER 4

IMPACTION AND MEGACOLON

What Is Fecal Impaction?

One very common risk of stool withholding is fecal impaction—a condition of having so much built-up stool that it becomes physically impossible to pass. This usually requires an urgent trip to the doctor or emergency room for an experience that, I can assure you, neither you nor your child will soon forget!

As described in Chapter 2, one of the initial signs of stool withholding is soiling (encopresis). Soiling is also a strong indication that fecal impaction is imminent. Other signs of impaction include a distended abdomen, pain, bleeding from the rectum, loss of appetite, vomiting or even fever.[1]

Treatment for impaction begins with removing the blockage of stool. This may be done in several ways, including enemas, suppositories and/or gentle manual removal by insertion of a gloved and lubricated finger. For a young child in pain who doesn't understand what is happening or why, these types of procedures are extremely invasive and traumatic.

Once the blockage of stool has been removed, you will most likely be directed to perform a follow-up colon evacuation (clean out, or "disimpaction") program at home, which may involve enemas, suppositories and/or laxatives. The initial evacuation usually takes about three days, after which a long-term maintenance regimen must be followed. (See Chapter 5.)

What Is Megacolon?

If the stool-withholding cycle is left to continue for an extended length of time, additional complications are likely to develop. One complication that can cause permanent damage is megacolon. "Megacolon" refers to an abnormally oversized large intestine.

Although megacolon can occur due to other causes, it most often results from chronic over-accumulation of stool in the colon, forcing it to expand and stretch beyond its normal capacity. If the colon is abnormally stretched out day after day, month after month and year after year, it should come as no surprise that it may eventually lose its ability to shrink back down to its normal size. Just think of what multiple pregnancies can do to a woman's abdomen...

One of the unfortunate results of megacolon is loss of sensation (the feeling of needing to "go") due to extreme colon distension. Basically, the muscles in the colon become lazy and stop contracting. According to Stephen Borowitz, MD, "As stool withholding continues, the rectum gradually accommodates, and the normal urge to defecate gradually disappears... Chronic rectal distension ultimately results in both loss of rectal sensitivity and loss of urge to defecate which can lead to fecal incontinence."[2] Treatment options for megacolon depend on the cause, type and severity of the condition, so this is best addressed by a specialist such as a pediatric gastroenterologist.

Now that we have defined constipation and stool withholding, and discussed some of the most common complications that can result, it's time to learn about the many prevention and treatment options—some of which I recommend, and others I feel are best avoided.

SECTION III

HOW DO WE STOP THIS?

CHAPTER 5

INTRODUCTION TO TREATMENT OPTIONS

Laxatives, Stool Softeners and Bulking Agents

In the past, the word "laxative" was reserved for substances or medications that produced a bowel movement by irritation or stimulation of the colon. Today, these agents are classified as "stimulant laxatives," and the general word "laxative" has become a catch-all for any substance or medication that assists or promotes the passage of stool, either by stimulating, softening, lubricating and/or adding bulk.

In truth, there are many different classifications for substances designed to treat constipation: **laxatives** (stimulant, osmotic and lubricant), **stool softeners** (emollients) and **bulking agents** (the various fiber varieties). Some treatments serve more than one of these functions, so there may be some overlap. My advice is to not concern yourself so much with classifications as with choosing a protocol you believe is going to be the safest and most effective for your child, and following it consistently.

Although a poor diet, lack of exercise and power struggles over toilet training may well have launched this problem, once the stool withholding cycle has reached the serious stages described in this book, correcting these lifestyle factors alone will rarely be enough to reverse it. You need a combination approach.

As much as I am an advocate of avoiding prescription and over-the-counter treatments with children wherever possible, this is one of those instances where an exception seems in order. If there was a "quick fix" for this unfortunate predicament, I wouldn't have written this off-the-wall book. But the truth of the matter is that solving a stool withholding problem will take considerable attention, understanding, patience and perseverance on your part. And, it's going to require specific treatment.

A comprehensive treatment regimen usually begins with an initial colon clean-out (disimpaction) program, followed by a long-term maintenance program (generally at least six months).

The Initial Clean-Out

Many pediatricians recommend beginning your treatment regimen with a disimpaction (colon evacuation) program. This typically involves the short-term use of enemas, suppositories and/or higher dose oral "laxatives" (usually stimulants).

A colon evacuation program should only be undertaken under the advice and supervision of a doctor. He or she will choose the appropriate treatment substance, or combination thereof. Disimpaction typically takes three days, although for some individuals it may need to be repeated. After disimpaction, a maintenance program must be followed.

The most commonly used substances for disimpaction include **suppositories**, **enemas** and **oral "laxatives,"** some of which will simply be higher doses of whatever maintenance treatment substance the pediatrician recommends.[1]

Suppositories

A suppository is a small, bullet-shaped solid designed for rectal insertion. Suppositories contain a substance or medication that dissolves inside the rectum when exposed to warm internal body temperatures, releasing its active ingredients and promoting a bowel movement. For best results, insert a few inches deep inside the rectum using your smallest gloved and lubricated finger.

Suppositories for constipation typically consist of the active ingredients **glycerin** or **bisacodyl**. Both types work quickly, usually within 15-60 minutes of insertion. Glycerin suppositories come in pediatric packages such as **Fleet Pedia-Lax** (a company that manufactures a wide variety of pediatric constipation remedies). Glycerin suppositories can be purchased over the counter and are considered safe, with few (if any) side effects.

Bisacodyl suppositories such as Dulcolax are considered safe for occasional, short-term use in adults and children over the age of six, but may be used in younger children under the advice and supervision of a physician. Bisacodyl falls into the stimulant laxative category and may cause cramping and/or diarrhea. When used regularly, low blood potassium levels may result.

Enemas

Enemas are a valid option when a child is suffering from fecal impaction. An enema consists of a bottle or bag connected to a tube or specialized tip. The tip is lubricated and inserted gently into the anus, and the fluid in the bottle or bag flows into the colon. Although invasive (and for some, traumatic), enemas are extremely effective and generally safe. There is a small risk of physical injury if not carefully performed or if the child is protesting, squirming and kicking. Fleet Pedia-Lax manufactures pediatric enema kits that can be purchased over the counter.

An disimpaction enema can consist of warm water or one or more of the following substances: mineral oil, normal saline, sodium phosphate, hypertonic phosphate, or milk and molasses. This book cannot advise you on these because the type and amount used depend on the child's age, weight, severity of impaction and whether he has any unique health conditions.[2] Unless you have training, experience and a highly cooperative child, do not attempt to administer a home-made enema concoction without the advice and supervision of a qualified medical practitioner.

Oral "Laxatives"

Oral laxatives for disimpaction typically include bisacodyl tablets, polyethylene glycol (PEG) powders, senna, magnesium citrate, high-dose mineral oil, high-dose fiber therapy, or higher doses of whatever prescription or over-the counter substance(s) are being used for maintenance.

Bisacodyl tablets such as Dulcolax are usually given in a single dose and work in approximately eight hours. Bisacodyl is not recommended for children under the age of six except under the advice and supervision of a physician. The child must be capable of swallowing small pills without chewing. Allergic reactions are possible. Side effects can include cramping, diarrhea, electrolyte imbalance and low blood potassium.

Polyethylene glycol (PEG) powders such as MiraLAX used to be available by prescription only, but now are available over the counter. MiraLAX is one of the most commonly recommended constipation treatments among pediatricians and pediatric gastroenterologists. It can be administered in higher, more frequent doses for disimpaction as well as lower, less frequent doses for long-term maintenance. More detailed information on MiraLAX can be found in Chapter 7.

Senna is a natural, vegetable based stimulant laxative that has been used for centuries. Brand names include Senokot (safe for children over the age of two who can swallow tablets), Fletcher's (available as a root-beer flavored syrup) and Pedia-Lax Quick-Dissolve Strips (this product may be difficult to find at most national retailers). Senna is intended for occasional or short-term use only.

Magnesium is a difficult to absorb mineral that often causes loose bowels as a side effect. Magnesium supplements come in many forms, from the cheapest, lowest quality and lowest absorption form magnesium oxide to some of the higher quality and higher absorption forms magnesium aspartate, ororate and glycinate.

Magnesium citrate such as the brand name Citroma and Citromag is an osmotic saline laxative that some physicians will use for 2-3 days as part of a disimpaction protocol or as a bowel prep before colonoscopy. Magnesium citrate is also the active ingredient in the popular magnesium supplement product, Natural Calm. In high enough doses, magnesium citrate usually produces a bowel movement within 30 minutes to three hours. Side effects may include cramps, gas, nausea, diarrhea and with prolonged use, elevated blood magnesium levels.

Finally, high dose **mineral oil** and/or high dose **fiber therapy** may be used for 3-4 days as part of a disimpaction program. Details on giving mineral oil and fiber to children can be found in the next chapter.

Maintenance Plan

For maintenance, you will need to rely on one or more prescription or over-the-counter substances (laxatives, stool softeners, bulking agents and so forth)—administered at regular intervals on a daily basis—for a *minimum* of six months.[3] My own son's pediatric gastroenterologist told us to expect to stay on a maintenance program for the same period of time that constipation has been present. In our case, she said, we were talking *years!*

The thought of administering laxative-type substances to a child for long periods of time is often an uncomfortable one for parents—and for good reason. Most products state on the label "Do not use for more than 7 days" yet your pediatrician may be telling you to keep your child on it for much, much longer.

This book does not constitute medical advice, nor is it intended to dictate which treatments to choose or how long to administer them. In my *opinion*, attending to factors of diet and water intake, increasing exercise and using the most natural (least synthetic) treatment substances is preferable. However, my goal is to simply provide you with as much information as possible, so you can work *with* your child's physician in making the very best decision for his short and long-term health.

Sticking with the Program

No matter which treatment substance(s) you choose, the three main mistakes parents make that lead to unsuccessful outcomes are: 1) using smaller doses of the treatment substances than the doctor advised, 2) skipping doses or giving the treatment inconsistently, and 3) weaning off too early.

According to Anthony Cohn, MD, "Treatment usually needs to continue months or even years until the withholding habit has been overcome... An appropriate combination of encouragement, fluid, fiber and laxatives is required to achieve the desired effect. The main obstacle to treatment success is usually families being laxative-phobic and either not giving enough, or stopping them too soon."[4]

Stephen Borowitz, MD adds, "It is very important to educate the family that using laxatives continuously for months may be necessary. This is particularly true in toddlers, because many months may pass before the association between fear and defecation is extinguished. Caregivers should be reassured as to the safety of long-term laxative use, and the importance of persistent treatment should be strongly reinforced."[5]

S	M	T	W	T	F	S
✔	✔	✔	✔			
✔	✔	✔				

*No matter which substance or combination you choose, the idea is to create enough **softness, bulk and lubrication** to ensure relatively pain-free bowel movements, even if your child has been withholding for several days in a row.*

During the first week, be prepared for a few accidents. Your child will still be trying very hard to withhold but will eventually become physically unable. Although it's possible the very first bowel movement after the initiation of treatment may cause discomfort due to oversized stool already present in the colon, any subsequent bowel movements should slide out rather painlessly and effortlessly.

Your main goal right now isn't toilet training. It's lessening—and then eliminating—the pain-fear-avoidance cycle. Trust me, there is nothing you can *say* that will convince your child to stop being afraid of pooping. It's your job to *prove* it! The very first thing that must be accomplished is ending the pain. Once that has been accomplished, time and your consistent efforts will eventually take care of the rest (fear and avoidance).

The next chapter will describe the protocol recommended by Walt Stoll, MD. His "magic combination" has helped countless families overcome the constipation and stool withholding cycle over the past few decades. For those who prefer an alternative protocol, or whose pediatrician has prescribed one, Chapter 7 will explore the basics of several other commonly used treatments—both prescription and over-the-counter.

CHAPTER 6

THE
"MAGIC COMBINATION"

Dr. Stoll's Remedy

This chapter focuses on the constipation and stool withholding treatment protocol recommended for decades by Walt Stoll, MD, founder of the popular website *Ask Dr. Stoll*, author of *Saving Yourself from the Disease-Care Crisis* and co-author of *Recapture Your Health* and *Beyond Disease Care*.[1] Sadly, Dr. Stoll passed away in August, 2011 at the age of 74. He was one of the most pioneering and dedicated public health educators this country has ever known. You can read more about his healing philosophies in the Prologue of this book.

The two substances in the "magic combination" touted by Dr. Stoll to be both safe and universally effective in ending the vicious cycle of constipation and stool withholding once and for all are **mineral oil** (for softening and lubrication) and **fiber** (for softening and bulk).[2]

Before going into detail about each of these substances, it is important to understand that individual dosing requirements vary significantly and can only be determined through a process of trial and error. The good news is, there's no need to worry about overdosing or dependency because neither of these substances are true medications. The only side effect of giving too much of either is runny stools—not a bad trade off given your child's current situation—and, completely temporary.

Part I: Mineral Oil

The first substance in the "magic combination" is mineral oil. Mineral oil is a very old home remedy, having been used to treat constipation for over a century. Plain mineral oil is sometimes called liquid paraffin, liquid petroleum or white oil.

This odorless, tasteless, colorless oil is extremely in-expensive, has no stimulant effect, is not systemically absorbed and simply passes through the colon mechanically. Each dose of this "lubricant laxative" works by mixing with and coating the stool that is formed that day. This not only keeps the stool soft by preventing water reabsorption in the colon, it also helps it slide out of the body easily.

Unfortunately, being the oily, tasteless substance it is, few children will willingly take mineral oil straight from the spoon. Children are notorious for refusing to cooperate with eating, drinking and swallowing unfamiliar or unpleasant substances. For many families, it's a two-person job (one to hold him down, and one to squirt it in his mouth!). But it needn't be an all-out battle. Administering strange-looking, foul-tasting or suspicious items simply requires planning, creativity and cleverness on your part.

When it comes to mineral oil, you can either purchase a flavored, emulsified version known as Kondremul, or prepare your own flavored mixtures at home.

Kondremul

Kondremul is an emulsion containing 55% mineral oil. Being already mixed and flavored, it is a convenient first choice for parents whose children like the taste of mint. Kondremul's official description states: "a non-fattening microemulsion of mineral oil that promotes gentle, predictable regularity without cramping or bloating; safe and effective with a minty flavor that tastes good and is sugar free; contains no stimulants."[3]

Begin with two tablespoons of Kondremul every evening. Give *only* in the evening, at least two hours after the last meal and immediately before bed. Adjust the dose up or down nightly according to results. Don't be afraid to increase the dose each evening until loose stools result. Once that occurs, simply cut back to the lowest effective dose for maintenance.

Home-Made Concoctions

If your child isn't a fan of mint flavor, you will want to purchase the regular mineral oil. Toss it in the freezer until ice cold, then prepare a palatable mixture using your choice of either orange juice or flavored milk (or milk substitute) according to the following instructions.

To make the orange juice mixture, mix one tablespoon mineral oil with a few ounces of ice-cold orange juice, and shake, blend or whip it together until smooth. Adding a pinch of baking soda (¼ teaspoon or less) will help the oil and juice blend more smoothly.

To make the flavored milk mixture, mix one tablespoon of mineral oil with a few ounces of ice-cold chocolate or strawberry milk (or milk substitute) then shake, blend or whip it together until smooth.*

With both the juice and the milk, the coldness helps disguise the oiliness. Make the mixture as cold as possible by keeping your mineral oil in the freezer and using cold, refrigerated juice or milk. As with the Kondremul, give the mineral oil concoctions *only* in the evening, and immediately before bed.

TIP

1 tablespoon (TBSP) = 3 teaspoons (tsp)

For accuracy, use measuring spoons.

Before offering the oil for the first time, experiment and taste test various combinations for yourself. Vary the juice and milk amounts according to preference. Try to strike a balance between using enough juice or milk to disguise the oil, but not so much as to create more volume than your child will willingly drink in a few minute's time (while it's still cold).

Try to get your child motivated and excited by explaining all the benefits and rewards of taking this "special medicine" (Yay!). Serve the mixture immediately after its preparation, get a drink of your own, and encourage him to win a speed-drinking race.

* The starter dose for mineral oil is 1 TBSP. The starter dose for Kondremul is 2 TBSP because it is only 55% mineral oil.

Pre-planning and palatability are so important, because if he refuses to cooperate, or if he begins to scream or cry, *you must not force it!* There is a chance he could accidentally breathe some of the oil into his lungs. Inhaling mineral oil into the lungs can cause a very resistant aspiration pneumonitis (lipoid pneumonia).

WARNING: You must *never* force mineral oil into the mouth of a crying or resistant child! At the first sign of protest, stop the administration immediately and either rely on the fiber alone, or choose an alternative protocol.

Timing and Dosage

Inquiring minds want to know: "Why can't I give the mineral oil during the day?" You *can*, but it's not advised. The reason is simple. Mineral oil tends to carry the fat-soluble vitamins (vitamins A, E, D and K) right out with it, so there is a (small) risk of eventual vitamin deficiency with long-term improper use.

By giving the oil only in the evening, at least two hours after the last meal of the day and right before going to bed, vitamin loss will be kept to a minimum. According to Dr. Stoll, even if this advice were to be completely ignored, it would take about a year of incorrect use for any significant deficiency problem to occur. For added reassurance, consider giving your child a high-quality multivitamin supplement each morning.

Begin by administering two tablespoons (TBSP) of Kondremul or one tablespoon of mineral oil the first evening. Increase the dose nightly by two teaspoons (tsp) of Kondremul or one teaspoon of mineral oil until: a) your child is having at least two stools a day that are easy and painless to pass, and/or b) you begin to see oil floating on the surface of the water after he has a bowel movement.

Again, dosages vary widely. The correct dose of mineral oil for any person (of any age) is just slightly less than the amount needed to produce that floating oil effect. Once you see the oil, simply cut back the total dose about 10% for maintenance.

Part 2: Fiber

The next substance in the "magic combination" is fiber. Used with the mineral oil, a rapid and successful resolution of the stool withholding nightmare is practically guaranteed. Fiber falls in the category of bulking agents. By adding bulk and drawing water into the colon, fiber helps correct and regulate bowel function whether you have constipation *or* diarrhea.

Fiber comes from the non-digestible part of plant forms, which means it is not absorbed into the bloodstream. Fiber comes in both soluble and insoluble forms. Some forms tend to cause more bloating and gas than others. Being a natural product (as opposed to a drug), fiber is considered safe for long-term use unless your doctor has advised otherwise.

The FDA has required that all bulk fiber products contain a warning about the risk of choking due to inadequate fluid intake (causing product to swell in the throat). The likelihood of this is slim to none, unless perhaps you attempted to swallow a spoonful of dry fiber without water. To avoid any *possible* choking risk, instruct your child to drink an extra cup of fluid and remain in an upright position for several minutes.

The term "fiber" generally refers to products containing **psyllium husk**, **methylcellulose**, **inulin** or **wheat dextrin**. Of these, psyllium husk powders are the most economical per dose. However, since we are dealing with children, palatability is probably more important than cost. If it is within your budget, purchase several varieties of fiber products to find out which one(s) your child will take most easily.

Psyllium Husk Powders

Psyllium husk powders (such as Metamucil) come in plain and orange flavored varieties, both regular and sugar-free.[4] Most are ground very fine and are accepted by children when mixed with cold water, although they do require frequent stirring while drinking. Perhaps the greatest down side to this soluble fiber is that it will thicken and gel up fairly quickly after stirred into water, so it may not be feasible for a young child who hasn't yet learned how to "chug" an 8-ounce cup of fluid.

Daily use of psyllium husk fiber has been shown to lower total serum and LDL cholesterol levels, reduce the risk of heart disease, assist with weight/fat loss, prevent certain forms of cancer, and lower blood sugar levels helping to control diabetes.[5]

Side effects are generally rare. You may experience some gas and/or bloating in the beginning, but this usually subsides with a few days. If taking other medications, take psyllium at least one hour after as it may hinder the medication's absorption. It's possible to become allergic to psyllium after repeated use or inhaling the dust. The allergic reaction has the potential to be severe (anaphylactic shock).

Methylcellulose

Methylcellulose is a soluble, non-fermentable fiber product (such as Citrucel), available both as caplets or an orange flavored powder (both regular or sugar free) that you can stir into cold water.[6] Since I know of few preschoolers who can swallow pills, the powder is your best bet.

According to the product label, Citrucel is "the only fiber for regularity that won't cause excess gas." It generally takes between 12-72 hours for methylcellulose to take effect. However, when initially used in higher doses along with the mineral oil, results should occur much sooner.

Side effects with methylcellulose are rare, but could include mild abdominal discomfort and a sensation of fullness. Allergic reactions are possible, but less likely than with psyllium husk powders.

Inulin

Inulin containing products (such as Fiber Choice) come in regular or sugar-free chewable flavored wafers.[7] Although they are a bit more expensive per dose, they taste as good as candy and have no grit. Your child might even think he is getting a treat at each dose and ask you for more!

The fiber in inulin is both soluble and fermentable. In my

experience, this type of fiber produces significant gas. However, you may find that its pleasant taste and acceptability to children overrides this inconvenience. Inulin is also considered a "prebiotic" fiber, which means it helps support a healthy gut flora by nourishing the probiotic (beneficial bacteria) populations in the gut.

Wheat Dextrin

Wheat dextrin products (such as Benefiber) are a favorite of many.[8] Although also on the more expensive end, this soluble fiber powder won't thicken, is available in flavor-free varieties, and dissolves completely in beverages and soft foods such as applesauce and yogurt, *and* you can cook with it. It also recently became available in chewable, fruit-flavored wafers.

This type of fiber may be one of the easiest to disguise and slip into your child's foods and drinks throughout the day. There doesn't appear to be any unpleasant side effects. Although the amount of gluten it contains is practically negligible (small enough to be classified as "gluten free"), individuals who are extremely gluten sensitive may need to avoid this type of fiber or speak with a doctor first.

Timing and Dosage

No matter which type of fiber you choose, or combination thereof, Dr. Stoll recommended starting with at least *double* the highest daily dose on the container. Divide this total amount by three, giving your child one-third three times a day. With each dose of fiber, urge fluids—preferably water. If you are using the mineral oil simultaneously, you will need less fiber than if you are relying on fiber alone.

Like mineral oil, fiber is neither a stimulant laxative nor a medication. Fiber is present in many natural, whole foods. It simply passes through the system, moving the stool mechanically along with it. Unlike with medications that are absorbed systemically, there is no such thing as "adult doses," "child doses" or "overdosing" on either of these substances. The only possible consequence of too much is loose stools—easily resolved by reducing the dose (and far better than the large, hard stools your child suffered with previously).

Note the frequency and consistency of each bowel movement and increase the mineral oil and/or fiber doses daily until your child is having at least two easy and painless movements per day. Do not skip even one evening or begin to "wean off" until several months after the pain-fear-avoidance cycle has become a distant memory.

The "magic combination" described in this chapter has a long and successful track record. (See Testimonials in Appendix C.) However, some children will refuse the flavored mineral oil concoctions, some will refuse one or more of the various fiber varieties, and some parents are only comfortable using a prescription or over-the-counter treatment recommended by their pediatrician.

When it comes to ending the stool-withholding cycle, it's not as important *what* substance you use, but *how consistently* you use it. Some families are passionate about "keeping it natural," whereas others wouldn't dream of questioning the harshest of prescription treatments if they are "doctor recommended." In the end, it is up to *you* to decide what is best for your particular child.

If for any reason you choose not to use the "magic combination," you will find basic, researched information on the wide variety of other available options (both prescription and over the counter) in the next chapter.

CHAPTER 7

ALTERNATIVE PROTOCOLS

Following Doctor's Orders

The previous chapter described a safe and effective protocol for treating constipation and stool withholding—mineral oil and fiber. This "magic combination" was backed by Walt Stoll, MD, a physician with over thirty years of experience, a founding member of the American Holistic Health Association (AHHA), and an expert in both conventional and alternative therapies. His protocol has a successful track record and has been used by numerous parents who have happily reported their child's stool withholding has become a thing of the past.[1]

However, as a mom who has been through a major, longstanding stool withholding ordeal with her son, I know firsthand that some children will protest, resist or refuse one or both substances, particularly the mineral oil if not properly disguised. Although fiber alone *may* be sufficient when used in high enough amounts, some children will need additional treatment, or a different treatment altogether.

In addition, some of you may be fearful or skeptical of the "magic combination" because of the risk of pneumonia due to

51

mineral oil inhalation, or because your child's pediatrician or specialist has recommended a different (likely a prescription) protocol instead. If that is the case, be sure to use what the doctor recommends or prescribes exactly as directed. Do not use less than you were told, and do not try to wean your child off the treatment early.

This chapter will describe the remaining treatment options most commonly used today. As explained in Chapter 5, these substances generally fall into the categories of stool softeners, bulking agents and "laxatives." The term "stool softener" is self-explanatory. Bulking agents are fiber products (psyllium husk, methylcellulose, inulin and wheat dextrin), all of which were described in the previous chapter.

The word "laxative," however, is often loosely used an umbrella term for any substance that helps make bowel movements easier—including stool softeners and bulking agents (fiber). Technically, however, laxatives fall into three categories: **stimulant**, **osmotic** and **lubricant**.

The rest of this chapter describes these various alternative constipation and stool withholding treatments. The following list is for informational purposes only. It is neither an endorsement for nor a recommendation of any of these products or substances. Some are considered safe for long-term use, and some are controversial or lacking long-term data.*

* As always, please consult with your child's pediatrician or gastroenterologist before starting, stopping or changing any treatment regimen.

Stimulant Laxatives

Stimulant laxatives include **bisacodyl** (such as Dulcolax and Correctol), castor oil (such as Purge Concentrate), **senna** (such as Ex Lax and Senokot), **cascara sagrata** (such as Nature's Remedy), **buckthorn** and **aloe vera**.

Stimulant laxatives are generally reserved for bowel prep before medical procedures such as a colonoscopy, for occasional irregularity in adults, and, if your pediatrician recommends it, as part of an initial disimpaction program.[2]

Other than for short-term use, stimulant laxatives (including suppositories) are inappropriate solutions for constipation and can be habit forming. With repeated use, the colon becomes used to the laxative "kick" and may eventually become dependent (refuse to function) without it.[3]

Osmotic Laxatives

An osmotic laxative is one which works by attracting and/or keeping more water in the colon to ensure softer stools. Osmotic laxatives also promote peristalsis (colon contractions) due to the distension effect of the retained fluids.[4] Osmotic laxatives can be broken down into two types: **hyperosmotic agents** and **saline**.

Hyperosmotic agents include glycerin suppositories, lactulose, sorbitol and polyethylene glycol. Saline laxatives include magnesium citrate, magnesium hydroxide, magnesium sulfate and magnesium citrate. We will explore each type briefly.

Glycerin suppositories were briefly covered in Chapter 5. Glycerin suppositories such as Fleet Pedia-Lax can be purchased over the counter and are considered safe and effective for occasional or short-term use. Results occur within 15-60 minutes of insertion. They are generally free of unpleasant side effects.[5]

Lactulose is a non-digestible synthetic form of the sugar lactose, and reportedly has no toxic effect even when taken at overdose levels.[6] Common brand names of this osmotic laxative include Enulose, Kristalose, Constulose and Generlac. These formulas come as a sweet tasting syrup that can be mixed in water or juice. Side effects of normal dosing may include cramping and frequent, pungent gas. There is a small risk of electrolyte imbalance over time. With high doses, side effects may include nausea, vomiting, uncontrollable diarrhea and resulting dehydration.

Sorbitol is an osmotic laxative derived from sugar alcohols.[7] Like lactulose, sorbitol is not systemically absorbed, tastes very sweet and is usually well accepted by young children. It is available as a prescription under its original name, "sorbitol." Side effects are described in detail in the prescription package insert.

Polyethylene glycol (PEG) is a large molecule that is poorly absorbed which means it basically "passes through the system." Common brand names include MiraLAX, GoLytely, NuLytely, Glycolax, GoEvac, CoLav, CoLyte and TriLyte. These formulas come as tasteless, odorless powders that dissolve completely in liquids, making them virtually undetectable when added to your child's water or juice.[8] This type of laxative is usually well tolerated and very few side effects are reported, although long-term safety has not been firmly established. At very large doses (such as when used as a bowel prep for colonoscopy), cramping, bloating, nausea and vomiting may occur.

Magnesium hydroxide is an inorganic compound that can be used both as an antacid and an osmotic laxative. Common brand names include Phillips' Milk of Magnesia (white chalky liquid) and Fleet Pedia-Lax chewable tablets (watermelon flavor).[9] Magnesium hydroxide works by holding water in the colon, but also by stimulating the colon's motility. Common side effects include cramps and diarrhea. Less common and more serious side effects include allergic reaction, nausea, vomiting, loss of appetite, weakness, lightheadedness and faintness.

Magnesium sulfate is also known as Epsom salts. This bitter tasting white rocky powder can be mixed with water to create an oral solution. Magnesium sulfate is rarely considered a valid option for children due to its extremely offensive taste. Oral magnesium sulfate is suitable for occasional use only and generally not recommended for children under the age of six.[10] It does, however, make for a soothing soak in the bathtub!

Magnesium citrate is a supplemental form of magnesium that can also be used as a laxative. Common brand names include Citromag and Citroma.[11] Magnesium citrate is also the active ingredient in the popular magnesium supplement Natural Calm. Magnesium citrate is both an osmotic saline laxative, derived from magnesium salt of citric acid. Unlike the osmotic laxatives listed so far, magnesium citrate is absorbed via the small intestine. However, given that this form of magnesium is also used as a high-quality mineral supplement, systemic absorption is not considered harmful. Other than supplemental formulas like Natural Calm, magnesium citrate laxative formulas are not generally recommended for everyday use.[12] Common side effects include mild abdominal cramps, gas and nausea. High doses can cause persistent diarrhea that may result in dehydration.

Lubricant Laxatives

A lubricant laxative is an emollient that works by lubricating and softening the stool, helping it to "slide out" much more easily. Mineral oil is the key ingredient in all lubricant laxatives. It may also be found under the names white oil, liquid paraffin or liquid petroleum. Detailed information and directions for use can be found in the previous chapter.

Stool Softeners

Unlike other "laxative" type products, stool softeners do little more than their name suggests. They do not stimulate the colon, draw water into the bowels or lubricate the stool—they simply soften it. The key ingredient in stool softeners is docusate sodium (such as in the brand name Colace).[13]

Stool softeners are considered safe and generally produce a bowel movement in 12-72 hours. However, they are not recommended for simultaneous use with mineral oil or for long-term use except under the advice of a physician. Common side effects include nausea, bloating, gas, cramping and diarrhea.

Which Treatment to Choose?

As you can see, the number of options available for treating constipation and stool withholding are nothing short of overwhelming. The good news is, you certainly don't need to concern yourself with trying them all. My favorite protocol is Dr. Stoll's "magic combination." (See Chapter 6.) The two most common doctor-prescribed formulas seem to be lactulose and MiraLAX.

I have done my best to include, or at least mention, all the available substances and treatments that are on the market today for treating constipation and stool withholding. If your doctor has recommended a substance that was not described in this book, please let me know by contacting me at:

gatewaytobeing@cox.net

The more you attend to the lifestyle factors of a healthy, high-fiber diet, water and exercise, the fewer "laxatives" you will need to use, and the more quickly you will be able to wean off them altogether.

CHAPTER 8

MAINTENANCE PLAN

Accidents Will Happen

If you have been toilet training your child, please consider loosening the reins for the next several months. During this initial period of establishing the correct dosing for the treatment substance you have selected, it's only natural for him to continue refusing to "go." Despite every effort, he will eventually be physically unable to hold it in, much to his dismay, and will likely have an accident. This is hardly grounds for punishment and *not* an appropriate time to enforce previous toilet training goals.

Try to keep the *big picture* in mind at all times. While it would be nice to have a compliant little one who is fully trained by the age of three, that is a highly unrealistic expectation when it comes to a stool withholding child! The number one obstacle is the **pain-fear-avoidance cycle**, and addressing this problem from any other perspective will most likely lead to failure.

Day After Day

Once the correct maintenance dosages of your chosen treatment(s) have been established, it is crucial to remain consistent with the protocol for quite some time. Day after day, week after week, month after month, your child will come to realize that it is once again *safe* to pass stool. The psychological factors will eventually recede, but only if your diligence ensures pain-free movements each and every time.[1]

Be sure to read the section entitled "Sticking with the Program" that begins on page 35. Even after things seem to have normalized, it only takes *one* recurrence of painful stool to jump-start the problem all over again. For this reason, it is almost always a good idea to continue treatment for an additional six months *after* the withholding stops in order to allow the psychological fear and trauma component to completely pass, unless your doctor has recommended otherwise.

Once you are confident this vicious cycle is truly behind you, you can experiment with cutting the dosages by 25-50%. If you are using the "magic combination," cut the dose of only *one* of these substances in half. About one month later, if your child is still maintaining well, try cutting the dose of the other one in half. Continue cutting the dosages in this manner each month until the child is is maintaining regular, healthy bowel movements on his own.

When it comes to any *chronic* health condition, there is a big difference between a "treatment" and a "cure." Until or unless the root cause of constipation is addressed, any progress your child appears to be making will be temporary at best. That isn't to suggest treatments aren't necessary, but please view them for what they are—substances that can help to relieve symptoms.[2]

Any recurring constipation is most likely caused by lifestyle factors. In order to keep the bowels running smoothly, both children and adults need regular exercise, adequate water intake and a healthy diet of natural whole foods. The next section of this book will provide information and tips on how to implement these important lifestyle changes.

SECTION IV

HOW DO WE NEVER GO BACK?

CHAPTER 9

BOWEL TRAINING

That "Gotta Go" Feeling

Under normal circumstances, the body signals us pretty clearly when the "time" has come, if you know what I mean. Technically speaking, the muscles lining the colon begin to move the bowels, creating a sensation of pressure and urgency (peristalsis).[1] If you are near a toilet, you probably heed Nature's call and take care of business. However, if you are stuck in traffic or in the middle of a business meeting, you'll do whatever it takes to postpone the call. Likewise, a potty-trained child tries to hold it in when he either doesn't have access to a toilet or is simply too busy playing to want to go.

Of course, postponing or ignoring the call is a major way to set the stage for childhood constipation and stool withholding. That's why one of the most important aspects of long-term success is to help your child get back in touch with his own natural body rhythms by following a program designed to *retrain the bowels.*

"Bowel training" involves taking advantage of the times we are most likely to experience peristalsis.[2] One of the most natural times for a daily bowel movement is first thing upon waking. The other natural times are around 20-30 minutes after each meal. Begin requiring your child to sit on the toilet (or potty chair) for several minutes during these key times. After the first few weeks, you'll be familiar with his body rhythms so can reduce his sitting frequency, as will be explained toward the end of this chapter.

No Pressure, Just *Sit*

Keep in mind the goal isn't to force a bowel movement, but rather to simply *sit* on the toilet for a certain period of time. Based on your child's personality and tolerance level, choose a time frame of 5-10 minutes (of course, excusing him immediately if he should happen to "go").

The point is to reinforce your child's mind-body connection. Help him associate *waking* and *eating* with *toilet* and that "gotta go"

feeling with "pooping." If you make this a requirement and not a choice, you will see encouraging results within the first week.

It is important that you find ways to make bowel training toilet time pleasant. The last thing you want is a hissy-fit power struggle, so talk up this new plan in the most appealing way you can rather than just springing it on him by surprise. Make "fun" the name of the game.

Entice him to spend this time reading a favorite book, or purchase an exciting new book that he's only allowed to read while sitting on the toilet. Place a step stool at the base of the toilet for the best positioning and leverage.[3] To prevent impatience, provide a timer that you can keep on the bathroom counter. Children don't yet have a strong frame of reference for time, so being able to see each minute go by will make bowel training less overwhelming.

The Poo Poo Chart

Get your child excited about the program by providing sticker charts (we called them "poo poo charts") and/or small rewards. Again, it's no use trying to *force* your child to have a bowel movement. After all, you are dealing with a stool withholding child! Be prepared to comfort his fears and praise him for his efforts. Keep track of his bowel movements by recording the date, time and level of associated stress, fear or pain.

DATE	TIME	FEAR?	PAIN?	NOTES
8/8	7:15am	Y	Y	started Miralax yesterday
8/9	—	—	—	refused
8/10	6:30pm	Y	N	
8/11	8:45 pm	Y	N	"It didn't hurt!" ☺

After the first week or two, you'll have enough data to see a pattern. For example, you may notice that he has a bowel movement almost every morning upon waking, rarely if ever has another one after breakfast or lunch, but frequently has another after dinner. In that case, consider reducing his bowel training toilet sessions to twice a day at those particular times.

By following the healthy lifestyle guidelines outlined in this section, in addition to *diligently* following one of the treatment protocols described in Section III of this book, the chance of failure is slim to none! It may not be "easy," but it is easier than what you've been going through so far.

Stick to your guns, day after day, week after week. It takes approximately twenty-one days of consistent repetition to create a new habit for life! By planning ahead and heeding the advice in this chapter, hopefully your child will come to look forward to his bowel training time, and become one of many adults who keep a basket of reading materials near the toilet and actually appreciate this small slice of private time, relaxation and solace.

CHAPTER 10

GO PLAY!
(NOT VIDEO GAMES)

Little Couch Potatoes

News flash: Sitting around all day is one of the main underlying causes of sluggish bowels and constipation! Physical activity plays a key role in establishing healthy, regular bowel habits. Exercise encourages peristalsis, shortens the transit time and limits the amount of water that gets reabsorbed from the colon, keeping the stool soft and easy to pass.

Prior to the invention and popularization of cable television, video games and home computers, children spent the majority of their time playing outside. At the risk of being one of those "When I was a kid..." people, I remember spending all day, every day running, jumping, hopping, skipping, climbing, tumbling, biking, swimming, roller skating, skate boarding, playing ball, jumping rope, playing hopscotch, pulling wagons, swinging on swing sets... in addition to doing chores. Watching cartoons was generally a Saturday morning event, not a daily fix.

My own children's generation has been drawn in by the excitement of modern electronic entertainment such as television shows, DVDs, video games, computer games, online chatting, text messaging and social networking. And, who can blame them?

There's nothing intrinsically "wrong" with electronic fun, but I think it's sad when parents don't encourage balance. Some families don't think twice about using electronics as a babysitter. The young child's brain is highly programmable. Concern over what they are exposed to is valid. Plus, the next thing you know, the kids are literally addicted to this stuff—they literally can't stop! Do you really want to set up patterns of obsessive/compulsive behavior as well as emotional outbursts and psychological withdrawal when the activity is denied?[1] Enough said. Off my soap box (at least for now)...

Childhood Obesity Risks

Another danger of a lifestyle that revolves around sitting in front of a screen comes from its sidekick, junk food. The common result? Childhood obesity is at an all-time high.

Picture your child, unnaturally inactive and sedentary for hours on end day after day, coupling his screen time with greasy, sugary, salty, processed snack foods such as chips, pizza, cookies, candy bars, fruit snacks and soda. Just because we've become a society where "everybody does it" don't be lured into a false sense of security that it is all in "fun" and therefore, harmless. Nothing could be further from the truth![2]

Granted, this is not specifically a book on parenting or child development. Yet these factors of diet and lifestyle *must* be addressed in a book about reversing constipation and maintaining healthy digestion. Who determines how much time per day (or week) your child spends playing with his electronic gadgets? Who determines what he's allowed to eat, and when? You, or him? If you, are your ultimatums respected or simply empty threats?

It's natural for children to try to get their way. They'll go so far as to say they hate you (which stings, and works with parents who buy into it). But believe it or not, children actually feel *more* safe and *more* secure with adults who calmly and consistently make it clear who's the boss. Create rules, limits and boundaries that best work for your family, then enforce them without backing down.

Don't assume your child isn't sneaking video game or computer time when you're not looking. Show him that you are paying attention by setting a timer and/or creating a chart to keep track and show you mean business. During the times of day when electronics are out of the question (and the chores and homework are complete), he'll attempt to convince you he's unbearably *bored*. But when the electronic options are removed, you'll be surprised how many fun and active things he'll find to do (like going outside and playing with the hose or riding a bike).

Leading by Example

Whatever goals you set in the short term, ultimately you'll want to keep your child's *long-term* health and well-being in clear focus. At the risk of offending anyone, here's a few valid questions you may want to ponder (or not...): If he continues living his current lifestyle, will he grow up to be a strong, self-disciplined, healthy, independent adult? Or, is he more likely to grow up to be an overweight, chronically ill, lazy individual who has no passion for life and no goals to pursue?

Believe me, I understand getting kids to lead a disciplined and organized life is easier said than done. It's a rather hopeless pursuit in families with parents who aren't willing to lead by example. If you are a couch potato, don't be surprised if your kids are little tater tots.

Model the behavior you want your child to adopt. Ride bikes and go on hikes together as a family. Go to the park. Sign your child up for youth team sports, tennis lessons, martial arts and dance classes. Get involved in boy scouts and girl scouts. If you have a gym membership, use it regularly—even if your child is too young to go, he will see that exercise, fitness and health are important to you.

CHAPTER 11

TOUGH LOVE DIET

My Kid Won't Eat That!

It's no surprise that certain foods contribute to dis-ease and chronic constipation, and certain foods contribute to health and regularity. Most people are aware that fiber plays a key role, but few people know how much fiber they need and which foods naturally provide it.

I've seen it time and time again, parents who throw up their hands in resignation because they believe they cannot get their children to drink plain water or eat healthy, natural foods. Children are clever little beings who are experts at convincing their exhausted parents they would rather starve than eat foods like green vegetables, brown rice, whole grain bread, oatmeal, high fiber cereals, unpeeled apples, unpeeled potatoes, raw nuts and seeds, baked chicken breasts, fish and so forth.

Who's in Charge, Here?

The fact is, children can only control their diet to the degree that parents allow. Period! They do not drive to the store, purchase the food or cook the food, so the only way they can eat an unhealthy diet is by convincing you to buy it, make it or give it to them. Just because a child throws himself on the floor after being told no doesn't mean you need to give in to him.

My oldest son entered the world with a mind of his own and a resolve that would challenge any new mom. When things didn't go his way, I was at a loss, not wanting to create a scene. I remember my great grandmother watching with dismay as I did my best to control my screaming child after telling him it was time to come inside for dinner. Concerned that I would end up with a juvenile delinquent, she sent me a book by Dr. James Dobson called *The Strong-Willed Child.*[1] The most valuable thing I learned was the following: When you give in to your protesting child to "keep the peace," you teach him that whining and crying gets him exactly what he wants.

Getting that one concept through my mind changed the entire dynamic of my family from that moment forward. I stopped rewarding my kids for negative behavior. I didn't resort to raising my voice, making ultimatums and so forth. I simply set the rules, calmly communicated them and let them know what the consequences would be if they chose not to comply. I was consistent and matter-of-fact (rather than shaming and angry) when the rules were broken. We have since enjoyed a loving, peaceful household with children who get along and speak to us and one another with compassion and respect.

How does this tie in with kids and food? For one thing, when you frequently use junk food as a reward (and withholding it as a punishment), you just might create a counterproductive dynamic with food that can last a lifetime.

You would be surprised just how quickly children will fall into line and eat a healthful diet if no other choice was offered. Fast foods and "junk" foods have their place, and are admittedly fun to eat, but they were never meant for ever-day consumption.

It is up to you to decide how much junk food your child should be allowed to eat on a daily or weekly basis. Create a plan and some rules, then follow through without wavering. Your child will protest at first, but soon enough, will come to enjoy the healthier foods and will eventually respect and appreciate you for offering them.

More of This, Less of That

A general rule of thumb is to focus on selecting and preparing foods that are whole, natural, unprocessed and unrefined. In addition, since we are focusing on the prevention and treatment of constipation and stool withholding, you will want to select foods that are high in fiber.

High-fiber foods (more than 7 grams per serving) in alphabetical order include: avocados, black beans, bran cereal, broccoli, brown rice, green peas, kale, kidney beans, lentils, lima beans, navy beans, oats, pinto beans, raspberries, soybeans and split peas.[2]

Medium high-fiber foods (more than 3 grams per serving) in alphabetical order include: almonds, apples (unpeeled), bananas (though these tend to be constipating), blueberries, cabbage, cauliflower, corn, figs, flax seeds, garbanzo beans, grapefruit, green beans, olives, oranges papaya, pears (unpeeled), pistachios, potato skins, prunes, pumpkin seeds, sesame seeds, spinach, strawberries, sweet potatoes, swiss chard, whole wheat pasta, winter squash and yams.[3]

"Fiber-rich" foods (less than 3 grams per serving) in alphabetical order include: apricots (fresh or dried), asparagus, beets, brussel sprouts, cantaloupe, carrots (raw), cashews, celery, collard greens, cranberries, cucumbers, eggplant, kiwi, mushrooms (raw), mustard greens, onions (raw), peanuts, peaches, peppers (sweet), pineapple, plums, raisins, romaine lettuce, summer squash, sunflower seeds, walnuts, whole wheat bread and zucchini.[4]

Foods to avoid include all refined, processed, canned and boxed foods, dairy products (milk, cheese, ice cream, etc.), processed meats, fried foods, white breads, white rice, non-whole grain crackers, cereals and pastas, and of course "junk" foods such as pizza, burgers, fries, chips, candies, pastries and so forth.

Ending the Food Battle

There is no need to demand, threaten, force or bribe a child to eat a particular food, and no need to punish a child who refuses. Avoid engaging in a high-drama battle by remaining calm, yet *firm*. Do not, under any circumstances, back down and give the child an old favorite to eat after offering a plate he refuses. Simply continue to affirm, calmly and matter-of-factly, that the only two choices are to either eat what is being offered or be excused from the table. No harm will come to even the most stubborn child who refuses to eat for several days. Your child will never truly starve himself!

Again, this is not a book on child psychology, but rather a

discussion on the factors that pertain to constipation and stool withholding. Therefore, rather than looking for a short-term "diet," focus on slowly incorporating a long-term lifestyle change. Get the entire family on board with the new healthy eating plan. To avoid temptation, either get the "junk food" out of the house or ration it carefully as an occasional treat.

As Dr. Stoll so often said: "When parents and caregivers remain firm, and the child *knows* they won't back down, the "battle" will pass rather quickly and the child will begin to taste (and eventually truly enjoy) the new foods. This aspect of 'tough love' will pay off for the rest of the child's life. If new parents had the proper information to attend to dietary factors that prevent constipation, beginning at weaning, they could avoid ever having to deal with the nightmare of having a stool-withholding child."[5]

CHAPTER 12

DRINKING
PLAIN WATER

Stop the Flavored Madness

Many children refuse to drink plain water, insisting on milk, juice and soda instead. The aggressive marketing of flavored drinks on TV doesn't help. Pure, clean water is *starting* to be promoted as a "cool" and healthy choice, but babies who were never given plain water in their bottles, or were given the fruit juices and purees at a very young age, have already become accustomed to "sweet." Parents can mistakenly believe they have no choice but to give in to their child's demands for flavored drinks, fearing the child will become ill or dehydrated if only water were offered. Let me tell you—been there, done that.

The importance of drinking pure, clean water on a daily basis cannot be understated.[1] Allowing your child to drink only milk, juice, soda and artificially sweetened flavored and colored drinks—no matter how "happy" it seems to make him—is doing him a great disservice. Imagine the potential long-term repercussions of reduced health if this habit is allowed to continue. Chances are you *know* this, you just don't know how to get your child on board.

One Ounce at a Time

The following is a method that will not fail to work unless you are weak in your resolve. I have used this method with one of my own sons, as well as in my work with young children on the autism spectrum who also refused water. In all cases, the child not only learned to accept water, but actually grew to enjoy it (and ask for more).

Before you begin, explain to your child that drinking water is very healthy and that it is an important part of becoming a big boy or girl. As a fun project together, create a water-drinking sticker chart using colorful markers. Purchase a box of kid-friendly disposable bathroom cups (the 3oz. or 5oz. ones) with favorite cartoon characters or designs, or let your child select a new, special reusable cup that will be for water only. If you choose the latter, be sure to stick to the rule that nothing besides water will ever go into this special cup.

Depending on the level of your child's water-drinking resistance, fill your child's cup with one or more ounces of good-tasting, filtered, cold water (if your tap water tastes awful, avoid it). The more resistant the child, the less water you will want to begin with. Fill another cup to the brim for yourself.

Sit your child down at the table (or in the high chair) and be sure to sit with him. Offer the little cup of water with the instructions that whoever drinks the water "all gone" can get up and go play. Make sure you are very clear that neither of you will be allowed to get up until your respective cups are empty. Notice whether your child begins to drink willingly. If he does, praise him in an excited, happy manner. If not, show him how quickly and easily you can drink your water by saying, "Watch this!" and pouring it down. Then say, "Look, I can get up now. Your turn!"

If you have other children in the house (or even adults) who willingly drink water, ask them to join efforts with you for "water time." Have several children and adults sit around the table together and give each of them a small serving of water, announcing to all what the rules are. "Whoever finishes their water first gets to go play first. Ready, set, go!" Your water-refusing child will see all the other people swallow the water immediately and leave the table, which will make him much more likely to do the same.

Stand Off: Who Will Win?

If your child still refuses to drink the water, be prepared for a waiting game. Do not leave the room, because if you do he will get up and sneak away. Continue to state the rules in a matter-of-fact manner. He will likely begin to whine and tell you how much he hates water and how much he really wants (or *neeeeeds*) to get up and go play. Don't react to the protests or crying, other than to repeatedly affirm, "As soon as you drink this all gone, you may go." Smile, remain calm, be pleasant. Do not raise your voice, and do not back down under any circumstances![2]

In other words, teach your child that there is one way, and one way only, that he is going to be allowed to get up out of the chair and go play—and that is to drink the water. If you have followed my instructions and knew you were dealing with a particularly strong-willed child, you will have given him only one ounce of water on the first day. This is such a miniscule amount, you certainly aren't expecting too much of him and, no matter how much drama he may attempt to unleash, there is no believable excuse he can offer as to why he "can't" drink it. Even if he says, "But I need to go pee!", do not allow him to get up until he swallows the water. This is one stand off you must win!

Repeat this process at least once a day, increasing to several times a day once you see that your child has given up the battle and is willingly drinking the water each time it is offered. Once you have gotten through the initial phase, you can continue increasing the water amount and begin adding additional rules such as "No juice until after you drink your water." In addition, it's a good idea to start diluting your child's juice little by little until it's about 50% water.

Half Your Body Weight

Your eventual goal is a child who willingly drinks the appropriate amount of water for his size each and every day. To determine the correct daily amount (for any person), take the body weight in pounds and divide it in half. Drink this amount in ounces per day. For example, a 48-pound child would need to drink 24 ounces of pure water per day (other drinks such as juice do not count).[3]

My youngest son was so stubborn about his hatred for water, our first session at the table took nearly two hours and involved a great deal of crying. You would have thought I was forcing him to swallow a nasty cough syrup. Within the first week however, repeating this process each and every morning, he gave up the struggle and simply swigged the water down quickly and went on with his day. Once the child accepts it, it's no big deal.

Over the next few weeks, I increased the amount of water in the cup at each sitting, until he was drinking 4 ounces at a time, three times a day. Although this still wasn't enough daily water for his body weight, it wasn't long before we accomplished our goals. Today, he drinks a 20-ounce bottle in the morning, a 20-ounce bottle after lunch and a 20-ounce bottle in the evening. This is in addition to the occasional milk, juice, soda or sport-type drinks.

One of the children I cared for had a similar stubborn distaste for water, and after receiving permission from his mother, I followed the same protocol just given. He loved picking out a sticker from my vast sticker collection and putting it proudly on his chart. He went from hating water to reminding *me* that it was "water time." Unfortunately, there was little follow-up at home and his parents remained convinced that for them, he would only drink cranberry juice. They seemed puzzled that he would happily drink water for me and not for them, but they held to their belief that there was nothing they could do about it.

APPENDICES

APPENDIX A

MAKE A LIST, CHECK IT TWICE

I know you don't want to let one more day go by before taking *some* kind of action to end the stool withholding nightmare. However, before embarking on the "formal" journey of presenting a firm plan of resolution to your child, I strongly advise you to read this book from cover to cover, and use the checklist that begins on the next page.

As stated earlier, when parents' expectations are reasonable and the follow through is consistent, children become much more secure, calm and willing to cooperate. A frightened, stool withholding child needs that consistency and that feeling of security more than ever. Parents who say one thing and do another, make empty threats, are inconsistent or give in at the first sign of struggle aren't doing their children any favors.

Using the following checklist as a guideline, create a plan of action. Get other family members, caregivers and teachers on board. Gather all your supplies *before* explaining all the new rules to your child. Then, follow through with consistent action, day after day, week after week, month after month, until this entire ordeal is nothing more than a distant memory.

Checklist

___ See the pediatrician if necessary.

___ Choose and obtain the treatment substance(s):

We will use _____

_____

_____

___ Purchase diapers again if necessary.

___ Obtain one or more fun children's books for toilet time.

___ Obtain a step stool the correct height for leverage and place it in front of the toilet.

___ Obtain a timer for the bathroom.

___ Obtain a notebook to track all treatments given (day, time, type, amount, side effects) and all bowel movements (date, time, size, consistency, pain, fear, etc.)

___ Create a reward "sticker chart" and post it on the bathroom wall. Be sure to have some favorite stickers on hand.

___ Type up your plan/schedule. Keep several copies on hand for caregivers (family members, babysitters, teachers, etc.)

___ Our bowel training schedule will be:

_____

_____

_____

___ Our child will drink ___oz. pure water per day. Our water drinking strategy is: _____

_____

_____

_____

___ Our child will eat at least ___ servings of the following high fiber foods each day: _____

_____

_____

_____

___ Our child will limit consumption of the following "junk" foods to ___ per week: _____

_____

_____

_____

___ Our child will be physically active each day in the following ways: _____

_____

_____

_____

___ Our child will limit the amount of time spent watching TV, playing video games, using the computer, etc. according to the following plan: _____

_____

_____

_____

HOW TO HAVE THE "BIG TALK"

Now that you have read this entire book (you *have*, right?), created an individualized plan you feel good about and gathered all your supplies, it is time to have a formal sit-down talk with your stool-withholding child.

Keep in mind you are about to impose a *significant* change in your child's normal routine, as well as your entire family's. Be sure to present your plan in the most positive light possible, emphasizing the rewards and the fun aspects of the new routine (picking out a new book, using the sticker chart and timer, etc.) rather than focusing on its restrictions.

Do not make your child feel he has done something wrong or present your plan as if it were a punishment for bad behavior. Emphasize your confidence that the plan will stop the pain and fear once and for all, and focus on praising him for his efforts every step of the way.

The following is an example of how I, personally, might have the "big talk" with a stool withholding child. Adjust your own words according to your child's age, level of understanding, personality, and so forth:

Sweetheart, I know that you have been feeling afraid to go poo poo because sometimes it hurts. Pooping isn't supposed to hurt. What would you say if I told you I know how to fix it so it won't ever hurt again? [You do?] Yes, I just read this great book called "Scared to Poop." It's all about this problem and how to fix it. Let me show you. (Show this book.)

And look, I got this "special medicine" that you are going to take every day. (Show the mineral oil and fiber or alternate substance.) *I tried it and I think it tastes good. This "special medicine" will make your poops softer and smaller so they don't hurt at all when they come out. And you know what else? [No, what?]*

I made this really cool sticker chart and bought your favorite stickers. And, I got you a cool new book to read. Do you want to see? [Yes!] Come with me to the bathroom. Every time you sit on the potty, you will put your feet on this really cool step stool. We will set this timer for 5 minutes, and you will get to look at your brand new book. [Cool... but I'm scared to go poop!]

That's OK sweetheart, I know you are scared. But you don't <u>have to</u> go poop when you sit on the toilet. You can just sit and enjoy your book until the timer goes off, and then you can go play again. If you DO make a poop, you *get to put a sticker on your sticker chart. [Whoa, Sponge-bob!] Yes, and remember, you have "special medicine" now so pretty soon, pooping will be easy!*

Now, follow me to the kitchen. I got some great new snacks for you. These snacks will also help the poo poo to stay soft and come out easier. You can still have some of your old favorite snacks sometimes, but just not every day. And we are all going to be drinking more water from now on. Water is the very best drink for people and pets. Do you ever see [your pet's name] drink soda or juice? [No!] That's right, because dogs/cats are very smart.

[I can't drink juice anymore?] You can, but just not all the time. And look, I got you this special cup just for water. [Cool! It's got my name on it!] That's right, drinking water will be fun! You know what else will be fun? We are going to ride bikes, play ball and go to the park more often. [We are?] Yes, because exercise is very important, and I really like spending time together as a family.

Are you ready to start our new plan? [Yes!] Great. I'm so proud of you. Do you have any questions?

I hope you found this sample talk helpful. Try to strike a balance between giving him just enough information but not overwhelming him with too much information. If your child is highly resistant to certain aspects (such as water drinking), you can de-emphasize those aspects at first.

You now have all the information and tools necessary to ensure a successful resolution to the constipation and stool withholding cycle. It has been my honor to write this guidebook. If you found it helpful, please be so kind as to write a positive review or testimonial on amazon.com. I wish you and your family all the best!

APPENDIX C

TESTIMONIALS

The following are excerpts from the "Ask Dr. Stoll" online bulletin board archives. Names are withheld to protect privacy. Walt Stoll, MD was the author of *Saving Yourself from the Disease-Care Crisis*, co-author with Jan DeCourtney of *Recapture Your Health*, and co-author with myself of *Beyond Disease Care*.

* + * + * + * + * + *

We have very recently overcome the same problem with our 3 ½ year-old. The mineral oil/fiber combination was a miracle for us. After a year and a half of withholding he is now not only pooping every day, but he goes to the toilet by himself to do it. And just one month ago we were ready to take him to the hospital! I hope you will have the same result as we've had.

* + * + * + * + * + *

I just wanted to let anyone whose child has been suffering know to follow Dr. Stoll's advice. My 2 ½ year-old child became very constipated when our family recently moved. My husband and I spent many hours in the waiting room at our doctor's office only to be hastily brushed out the door with no real explanation as to why this was happening and what we could do about it. When I read Dr. Stoll's article on constipation and stool withholding, it made sense and three weeks later my son is doing much better. He still has the psychological fear of a painful bowel movement, but after he passes stool he smiles and says, "That didn't hurt, now my bum will feel better." As a parent I never thought I would be so happy to hear those words from my child. There is nothing worse than watching your child suffer, I am so grateful that this worked.

The stool withholding protocol *works*, but you have to follow it faithfully and consistently, and give it in sufficient amounts. Don't be afraid of the suggested dosages because these are *not* laxatives and cannot cause dependency! My son refused the mineral oil and I could not risk him inhaling it so that wasn't an option for us. I gave him Fiber Choice chewable orange wafers in the daytime and Metamucil "cookies" in the evening with a glass of (diluted) juice with buffered vitamin C powder stirred in (the C also loosens stools and has the added benefit of enhancing the immune system). These he accepted. But that is only half the battle. The most *important* thing was getting him to drink plain *water* (which he refused before). I had to get real tough to do it, but now he drinks a 24-oz. bottle of water every day without a fuss. We set up reward systems and "poo poo charts" (with stickers)—anything and everything I could think of. It was very important to sit him on the pot right after each meal. We got an electronic book called *I Know Where My Food Goes* which explained how food moves through the digestive tract. Diet is so important too. I gave him lots of broccoli, blueberries, apples, asparagus, etc. If we can do it, you can do it! Now he is off everything and goes almost every day without any pain or fuss. We finally won. This is so important, it has to be your full time job until it is solved.

I am forwarding Dr. Stoll's article about stool withholding in children to my pediatrician and posting the link on all relevant discussion boards because his system works! My son always had a slow colon, as does his father and grandfather. As an infant we had no complaints—we had to change a poopy diaper only once a week. Our pediatrician assured us that this was normal. But over time, as his stools became larger and dryer, he began to withhold. By age four he would stumble around like a little stick man rigid from the strain of constant withholding. His peers shunned him. The advice of pediatricians, other parents and literature was useless. On occasion, we had to resort to enemas. Finally, I found Dr. Stoll's article and intuitively felt it was the right thing to do. After a few days, my son began to have regular, if small, bowel movements. After six weeks, he passed his first normal stool in two years. We are continuing on the program and are basking in the greatly improved quality of our lives.

* + * + * + * + * + *

I know how worried parents are when their children are withholding, and I just want to let them know that there is a light at the end of the tunnel if you are patient and don't push too hard with the toilet training. There were no more problems with fissures, hard stools, etc. after my daughter started taking the mineral oil and Metamucil; and that was very important. It took about six months for her to realize that it didn't hurt when she pooped, but she always was a little fearful. Hope this helps someone. I do thank Walt, especially, and also all the other parents who answered my posts about this.

* + * + * + * + * + *

I stumbled upon this website two weeks ago when I was at my wit's end trying to find a solution to my three-year-old's constipation problem. She had been suffering from this problem for awhile and her situation had been getting worse and worse. There were times when she had no bowel movement for 8 days. Her mood would get very cranky and we'd spend whole days at home when she'd do her 'dance' running around, pulling up her knees to her tummy, holding it in. It was torturous watching her go through this. She'd have to skip school because she was in such misery. The doctor was useless. I was under the impression that this was a very rare case. All my daughter's peers are potty trained and no constipation problems at all. Anyhow, your website was a God-send. Trust me, it works, it does require patience though. I've not felt so happy in a long time. I just want to thank everybody on this board who shared their insights and tips. Our story is proof that fiber and water and some oil really help solve this problem. Thanks everyone!!!

* + * + * + * + * + *

PROLOGUE

This book is an offspring of one of the chronic health conditions covered in *Beyond Disease Care*, which I co-authored with Walt Stoll, MD.[1] Through my years of writing for Dr. Stoll, as well as through my own personal research and challenges with chronic health conditions, I have gained incredible knowledge and experience that I feel compelled to share with others who are suffering.

Constipation and stool withholding in children is perhaps one of the most needed yet least talked about topics among the medical community—including both conventional and holistic practitioners. Having gone through this ordeal with one of my own children, I'm so grateful to also have had the opportunity to work with and learn from Dr. Stoll, the first person who to successfully present me with the "big picture" when it came to symptoms, health and dis-ease.

In closing, I would like to share with some of you the most important core insights I gained from co-authoring *Beyond Disease Care* with Dr. Stoll, and explain how these insights relate to the topics of constipation and stool withholding.

1. It is important to understand the difference between an "acute" health condition and a "chronic" health condition. An acute health condition can be defined as any illness or set of

symptoms that comes on suddenly and tends to be short-lived. A chronic health condition can be defined as any illness or set of symptoms that develops slowly over time, remains persistent or tends to recur. Both constipation and stool withholding tend to fall in the "chronic" health conditions category.

2. The word "treatment" is not synonymous with the word "cure." To truly prevent or cure any disease, you must address the root cause (the *why*) of that disease. A treatment refers to any number of remedies intended to temporarily alleviate the symptoms of an acute or chronic illness, injury or disease. A cure means healing a condition permanently by eliminating its root cause. When it comes to constipation and stool withholding, the use of laxatives, stool softeners and bulking agents are treatments, whereas addressing lifestyle factors of proper diet, exercise and water intake is the cure.

3. Symptoms are messages from the bodymind—if you do not heed the warning, be prepared for your bodymind to shout louder. In other words, the presence of constipation is letting you know that your body is not getting the proper diet, fluids and exercise it needs. If you do not heed this message by correcting constipation at its root cause, be prepared for additional chronic health problems to develop over time.

In general, you will find that conventional physicians will treat nearly all health complaints with the prescription pad, whereas naturopaths, osteopaths, chiropractors and other alternative health practitioners will recommend more natural or over-the-counter approaches. The decision whether to use conventional or alternative treatments (or a combination of both) is a personal one. My goal is to provide you with as much information as possible so you can make the most informed decision for your child.

To order your copy of
Beyond Disease Care

Please e-mail Kathleen at:
gatewaytobeing@cox.net

PRICE: $19.95

PayPal, money order or cashier's checks.
Type **Scared to Poop** as your subject line
to receive FREE shipping!

REFERENCES & RESOURCES

Introduction

1. Quotes Daddy. www.quotesdaddy.com.

Chapter 1

1. Dr. Jodi Judge, DC. Judge Chiropractic Center West. 14155 N. 83rd.

Avenue, Suite 102, Peoria, AZ 85381. 623-878-0475.

www.judgechirowest.com.

Colon Cleansing & Constipation Resource Center. A department of Global

Healing Center, Inc. 2040 North Loop West, Suite 108. Houston, TX

77018. Phone 800-476-0016.

2. American Academy of Pediatrics. Adapted from Fleet Pedia-Lax website.

Chart can be viewed online at: http://pedia-lax.com/constipation-

education/faqs.

3. "What Are Normal Bowel Movements?" BM-Bowel Movement. Article

available online at: www.bm-bowel-movement.org.

"How Often Should I Move My Bowels?" Konstantin Monastyrsky. Gut

Sense. Article available online at: www.gutsense.org.

4. Walt Stoll, MD and Kathleen M. Diehl. *Beyond Disease Care: When Your TREATMENTS Fail to CURE You...the Truth about How to Prevent and Reverse Today's Most Common Chronic Conditions.* Sunrise Health Coach Publications, October 2011.

5. "Constipation: What Causes Constipation?" National Digestive Diseases Information Clearinghouse (NDDIC). Article available online at: http://digestive.niddk.nih.gov.

6. "Constipation in Children." Robert J. Ferry, Jr., MD et al. E-Medicine Health. Article available online at: www.emedicinehealth.com/constipationin_children/article_em.htm.

   "Constipation." WebMD. Digestive Disorders Health Center. Article available online at: http://www.webmd.com/digestive-disorders/digestive-diseases-constipation.

   "Constipation." The Mayo Clinic. Article available online at: http://www.mayoclinic.com/health/constipation/DS00063/DSECTION=causes.

   "Evaluation and Treatment of Constipation in Infants and Children." Wendy S. Biggs, MD, et. al. American Academy of Family Physicians (AAFP). Feb 1, 2006. Article available online at: http://www.aafp.org/afp/2006/0201/p469.html.

7. "Pediatric Constipation Clinical Presentation." Stephen Borowitz, MD et al. Article available online at: http://emedicine.medscape.com/article/928185-clinical.

8. *See Chapter 1, Note 4.*

Chapter 2

1. "Toilet Training and Toileting Refusal for Stool Only: A Prospective Study. Bruce Taubman, MD. Article can be viewed online at: http://pediatrics.aappublications.org/content/99/1/54/abstract.

2. "Pediatric Advice: The Next Generation of Knowing." *Ask Lisa: Free Pediatric Advice.* Lisa Kelly, RN, PNP, C. www.pediatricadvice.net.

"Stool Soiling and Constipation in Children." Family Doctor.org. Article available online at: http://familydoctor.org/online/famdocen/home children/parents/toilet/166.html.

3. Jessica Williams. *Withholding: A Common Toilet Training Challenge.* Excerpt available online at: www.toddlerstoday.com.

Chapter 3

1. "Anal Fissures." Mayo Foundation for Medical Education and Research (MFMER). Article available online at: http://www.bing.com/health/article/mayo-126441/Anal-fissure?q=anal+fissure.

2. "What Is an Anal Fissure?" Sheila Jacobson, MBBCh, FRCPC. Article can be viewed online at: www.aboutkidshealth.ca/En/HealthAZ/ ConditionsandDiseases/DigestiveDisorders/Pages/Anal-Fissure.aspx.

3. "Fissurectomy as a Treatment for Anal Fissures in Children." G.F. Lambe, et. al. Article can be viewed online at: www.ncbi.nlm.nih.gov/pmc/ articles/PMC2503490.

Chapter 4

1. "Withholding Stool." Lisa-ann Kelly, RN, PNP, C. *Ask Lisa: Free Pediatric Advice.* Article available online at:

http://pediatricadvice.net/2006/07/withholding-stool.html.

2. *See Chapter 1, Note 7.*

Chapter 5

1. "Evaluation and Treatment of Constipation in Infants and Children." Wendy S. Briggs, MD and William H. Derry, MD. American Academy of Family Physicians (AAFP). Feb 1, 2006. Article available online at: http://www.aafp.org/afp/2006/0201/p469.html.

"Pediatric Constipation Treatment & Management: Colon Evacuation." Stephen Borowitz, MD et al. Article available online at: http://emedicine.medscape.com/article/928185-treatment.

2. Ibid.

3. "Stool Withholding." Anthony Cohn, MD. *Journal of Pediatric Neurology.* 2010. Adapted from *Constipation, Withholding and Your Child: A Family Guide to Soiling and Wetting.* Jessica Kingsley Publishers, 2006.

4. Ibid.

5. *See Chapter 1, Note 7.*

Chapter 6

1. Stoll, Walt MD. *Saving Yourself from the Disease-Care Crisis.* Sunrise Health Coach Publications, 1996.

Stoll, Walt MD and DeCourtney, Jan. *Recapture Your Health.* Sunrise Health Coach Publications, 2006.

Stoll, Walt MD and Diehl, Kathleen M. *Beyond Disease Care.* Sunrise Health Coach Publications, 2011.

2. Walt Stoll, MD. Ask Dr. Stoll: Information about Combining Conventional & Alternative Medicine. "Stool Withholding and Constipation in Children." Article available online at: http://askwaltstollmd.com/articles/cons.php.

3. Kondremul: Plain Liquid Lubricated Laxative. www.kondremul.com.

4. Metamucil: Multi-Health Fiber. www.metamucil.com.

5. "Psyllium Health Benefits." Home Remedies Web. Article available online at: http://www.homeremediesweb.com/psyllium-health-benefits.php.

6. Citrucel with Smart Fiber. www.citrucel.com

7. Fiber Choice Fiber Supplement. www.fiberchoice.com.

8. Benefiber Fiber Supplement. www.benefiber.com.

Chapter 7

1. *See Chapter 6, Notes 1 and 2.*

2. "The Dangers of Stimulant Laxatives." Global Healing Center: Natural Health and Organic Living. Article available online at: http://www.globalhealingcenter.com/stimulant-laxatives.html.

3. "Laxatives for Constipation: Stimulant Laxatives." John P. Cunha, DO and Jay W. Marks, MD. Medicine Net. Article available online at: http://www.medicinenet.com/laxatives_for_constipation/page5.htm.

4. "Before You Use Osmotic Laxatives for Constipation." Barbara B. Bolen, PhD. Article available online at: http://ibs.about.com/od/constipation/bb/osmoticlaxatives.htm.

5. Fleet Pedia-Lax Glycerin Suppositories. Information available online at: http://pedia-lax.com/products/glycerin-suppositories.

6. Lactulose. Drugs.com. Information available online at: http://www.drugs.com/pro/lactulose.html.

7. Sorbitol. Drugs.com. Information available online at: http://www.drugs.com/pro/sorbitol.html.

8. Miralax: Restore Your Body's Natural Rhythm. Information available online at: http://miralax.com/miralax/consumer/default.jsp.

9. Phillips' Milk of Magnesia. Information available online at: http://phillipsrelief.com/products/phillips-milk-magnesia.

Fleet Pedia-Lax Chewable Tablets. Information available online at: http://pedia-lax.com/products/chewable-tablets.

10. Magnesium Sulfate: Epsom Salts. Drugs.com. Information available online at: http://www.drugs.com/mtm/epsom-salt.html.

11. Magnesium Citrate: Oral. Citroma. Medicine.net. Information available online at: http://www.medicinenet.com/magnesium_citrate-oral/article.htm.

12. Natural Calm Magnesium Citrate Supplements. Information available online at: http://www.calmnatural.com/.

13. Colace: Docusate Sodium. PDR Health: Physician's Desk Reference. Information available online at: http://www.pdrhealth.com/drugs/colace.

Chapter 8

1. *See Chapter 6, Note 2.*

2. *See Chapter 1, Note 4.*

Chapter 9

1. "Peristalsis." Medline Plus. Definition available online at:

http://www.nlm.nih.gov/medlineplus/ency/article/002282.htm.

See also Chapter 2, Note 2.

2. "Potty Training for Children with Bowel Problems." Labor of Love. Article

available online at: http://www.thelaboroflove.com/articles/potty-

training-for-children-with-bowel-problems.

3. "Toilet Training Basics." B.D. Schmitt, MD. Clinical Reference Systems.

Article available online at:

http://www.sopeds.com/pedsadvisor/hhg/btoilbas.htm.

Chapter 10

1. "The Negative Effects of Television Addiction and Computer Addiction."

Parenting Healthy Children. Article available online at:

http://www.parenting-healthy-children.com/effects-of-television.html.

2. "Parents: Sedentary Lifestyle Leads to Child Obesity." Lauran Neergaard,

AP medical writer. Article available online at: http://napavalleyregister.

com/lifestyles/health-med-fit/article_185166C1-cfd2-55a8-8ef7-41b6

0a18a1.html.

Chapter 11

1. Dobson, James C. *The Strong-Willed Child.* Tyndale House Publishers, 1995.

Revised edition *The New Strong-Willed Child.* 2007.

2. "Foods High in Fiber and Fiber Rich Foods." Common Sense Health.

Article and list available online at: http://commonsensehealth.com/

Diet-and-Nutrition/High_Fiber_Food_Chart.shtml.

"List of High Fiber Foods." Colon Cleansing & Constipation Resource Center. List available online at: http://www.colon-cleanse-constipation.com/list-of-high-fiber-foods.html.

3. Ibid.

4. Ibid.

5. *See Chapter 1, Note 4.*

Chapter 12

1. "Why Drinking Water Is the Way to Go." Mary L. Gavin, MD. Kids Health. Article available online at:

http://kidshealth.org/kid/stay_healthy/food/water.html.

2. *See Chapter 11, Note 1.*

3. "How Much Water to Drink a Day?" Healthy Water. Article available online at: http://www.healthy-water-best-filters.com/how-much-water-drink-day.html.

"Daily Water Intake Calculator" tool available online at:

http://www.calculatorslive.com/daily-water-intake-calculator.aspx.

INDEX

C

encopresis (see soiling)

enemas, 23-24, 31, 32, 101

energy level, 4

Enulose, 54

esophagus, 7-8

exercise, importance of, 5, 13, 30, 35, 57, 60-61, 71, 73, 75, 97, 106

Ex Lax, 53

F

family support, xi, 13, 81, 91, 92, 95

fast food, 79

fatigue, 4

fear of bowel movements, 11, 14-16, 22, 36, 37, 48, 59-60, 68, 92, 95, 100, 102

fecal impaction, x, 14, 23-24, 30-34, 53

fever, 23

fiber, 5, 19, 30, 34, 35, 39, 43, 44-48, 51, 52, 57, 77, 79-80, 93, 96, 99, 103

Fiber Choice, 46, 100

fissure (see anal fissure)

fitness, 75

Fleet Pedia-Lax, 31-33, 53-54, 55

flu/influenza, 3-4

food allergies/hypersensitivities, 5-6

R

S

Y

Z

z y x w v u t, s r q p o n m, l k j i h g f, e d c b a!
(Learn the alphabet backwards, I dare ya!)